CATKU

CATKU

WHAT IS THE SOUND OF ONE CAT NAPPING?

PAT WELCH

**Andrews McMeel
Publishing**

Kansas City

ISBN-13: 978-0-7407-4169-2
ISBN-10: 0-7407-4169-1

Library of Congress Control Number: 2003112914

06 07 08 TWP 10 9 8 7 6 5 4 3

ATTENTION: SCHOOLS AND BUSINESSES

Andrews McMeel books are available at quantity
discounts with bulk purchase for educational, business,
or sales promotional use. For information, please write to:
Special Sales Department, Andrews McMeel Publishing, LLC
4520 Main Street, Kansas City, Missouri 64111.

Catku began as
an e-mail exchange between
Melissa Crowley and Heidi Delgros, in
Sacramento and San Jose, California, respectively.
The idea was theirs and they wrote the first Catkus,
many of which are included in the book. (So, okay, maybe
I owe them some money.) It's true that it was my idea that
it could be a book, and it is also true that I wrote the ninety
or so additional Catkus needed to make a book. And yes, the
illustration and design are mine, and of course it is not exactly
incidental that I have done two or three books in the past with
Andrews McMeel and that these highly regarded publishers hold
me in such esteem—well, that is to say they consider me . . . well,
they didn't actually remember me, but they were willing to
listen to the idea. Oh, and the title, that was mine, too. But
this is not about taking credit—though even a little book
like this is a lot of work—this is an acknowledgment
of the people without whose original concept
there would be no book at all: Melissa
Crowley; Heidi Delgros. It's a
kharma thing.

CATKU

THE TEMPLE

had been at the foot of the mountain for a thousand years.

At the moment of its four hundred thousand and first dawn, the student approached the master.

Master, how can we know if we are worthy of this existence?

Observe, there in the shadows, the temple cat. In this you will find your answer.

He is asleep.

True.

He is almost always asleep.

Also true.

He produces nothing, yet we feed him.

It is so.

He provides no service, yet we house him.

Yes.

He gives no sign that we matter to him.

None whatever.

And, unlike the temple dog, he makes no effort to curry our favor.

Correct.

Yet you say the answer to my question is in this cat.

So I have said.

No—not in the cat, but in my observation of the cat.

Don't overthink it, kid.

Then the answer is that we should imitate his disregard for earthly things—or is it that we should beware of such disregard—or that—that . . . Master, I am not worthy. I cannot find the answer in this cat.

But the temple's four hundred thousand and first sunrise had painted an oblique rectangle of sunlight on the courtyard and, in its exact center, the master had curled up and gone to sleep.

MY SQUARE OF SUNLIGHT   SHORT HOURS LAT

CAL WORLD

ER, IT HAS MOVED THUS THE WORLD ANNOYS

The food in my bowl
Is old, and—more to the point—
Contains no tuna.

Three a.m., silent.
Suddenly, six dogs barking.
No one here but me.

You open a book.
Flat, white, clean, smooth: like a bed.
Any more questions?

My day: first a nap

Then a leisurely dinner

Followed by sleeping.

You've bought a new toy

Money wisely spent on me.

I love the boxes.

So you want to play.

Will I claw at dancing string?

Your ankle's closer.

熟能生巧 Furiously climb,

Descend, and do it again:

Brand-new loose-weave drapes.

My claws need a trim.

But where? All has been shredded.

Except the new couch . . .

There's no dignity

In being sick—which is why

I don't tell you where.

My favorite place,

Dim, soft, snugly enclosing.

Whose sweater drawer?

The saltwater tank:

Calming, beautiful, to you.

I think of seafood.

Seeking solitude

I am locked in the closet

For once I need you

ON CLAWS: BEAR IN MIND

RETRACTABILITY IS

STRICTLY OPTIONAL

Your friend's sudden moves
And loud voice are amusing.
We'll be dumping him.

 Tiny can, dumped in
Plastic bowl. Presentation,
One star; service: none.

The big table: no.
But the sun makes a bed there.
The big table: yes.

I walk on this shelf.

No real destination, just

Love of crashing glass.

Morning rushing noise

You leave for work; it's quiet

I'll have a nice day.

The dog licks your face;

You laugh, gratified. His tongue?

I know where it's been.

Am I in your way?
You seem to have it backward:
This pillow's taken.

My dulcet mewing,
Your favorite sound. And mine?
The can opener.

Your friends are sneezing.
It seems they have allergies.
Who leaves, I wonder?

Scratch under my ears.

Alas, I like it *too* much.

This bite just won't count.

Your mouth is moving;

Up and down, emitting noise.

I've lost interest.

I stare; you stare back.

You think, I think she's thinking!

I think—well, nothing.

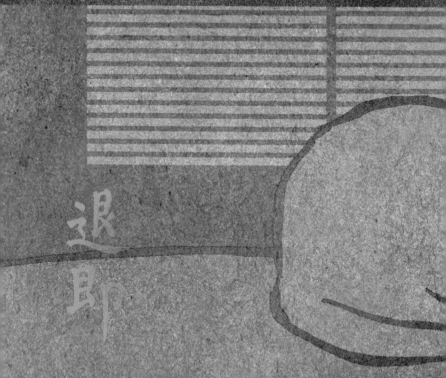

THE PATH OF E

FREEZING DAWN: YOU LEAVE I NOW SLEEP

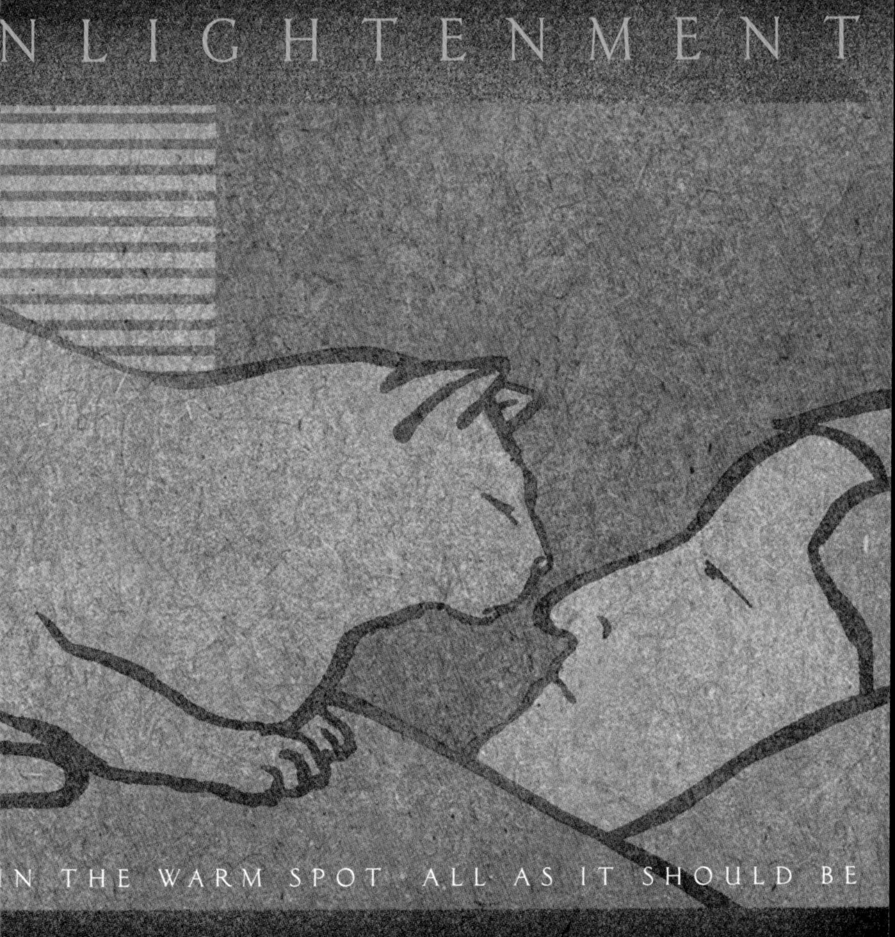
NLIGHTENMENT
IN THE WARM SPOT · ALL AS IT SHOULD BE

Touch me, touch me not.

This is not a guessing game.

The answer is claws.

Aloud you wonder

How I can sleep all day long.

While you yak, I can't.

You wish for a cat

Purring, companionable

I'm free next Friday.

Silence of the night
Broken by our raised voices.
Harmony—to us.

The dog wags his tail,
Seeking approval. See mine?
Different message.

Someone new comes in;
You want me to purr for them.
You do keep Band-Aids?

Strife, stress, and trouble.

How does the cat stay serene?

Simple trick: don't care.

The dog fawns; obeys.

Then you take him to the vet.

I'll stick with my act.

My brain: walnut-sized.

Yours: largest among primates.

Yet who leaves for work?

Can I really land
On my feet? Yes, but is your
Insurance current?

 You give me dry food,
Like gravel in a sandbox.
Perhaps I'll use it . . .

One room, one thousand
Apes: *War and Peace*. One thousand
Cats: *Do Not Disturb*.

THE CAT AND THE DOG

In a time closer to the beginning of time than now, the cat and the dog were the same and were not enemies. When they first saw men, the dog said, "That's an up-and-coming species. I wouldn't be surprised if they end up in charge of the whole thing. And I'll bet if I play my cards right, I can get them to take care of me."

The cat said, "What cards would those be?"

"Well, you have to give them something. I'll be loyal and friendly, and I'll do what they want."

"And for this you'll get what?"

"I'll never have to hunt, or find my own bed, or stay out in the cold."

"You'll never be free, or choose your own path, or howl your name at the moon."

"You're just jealous because it was my idea. I hadn't noticed until now, but you are a bitter and unprepossessing creature."

And the dog went and made his deal, and it was binding.

As time passed, the cat watched and saw that men huddled in the cold, scrabbled for food, and lived in fear of large sharp-toothed animals; they were not so impressive. He saw also that the dog was keeping his bargain. The next time food was placed before him, the cat walked in. Food was also put down for him. As they ate, the dog said, "You know, you will have to pay for this. Likely they will throw sticks or expect affection." The cat licked his chops and said, "I think not. You negotiated with a weak adversary without due diligence, and you have bound yourself unadvantageously. I, on the other hand, am as full as you are, but have signed nothing. The food here, by the way, lacks a certain something. I think I'll go see what's on at the next settlement."

The dog has not much liked the cat since then.

BIG DOG GROWLING; SMALL DOG YAPPING. WHA

Y · S P I R I T

績
幽

T IS THE SOUND OF ONE CAT SCRATCHING?

A home with a cat
Has no need of sculpture. But
It does need tuna.

Special furniture
For me? You needn't bother;
The silk chaise will do.

Visiting children:
Adorable, like kittens.
You may remove them.

The monk meditates;
The master enters his trance.
The cat takes a nap.

What is put outside
In the rain will soon return
To walk on the couch.

Earth is in balance:
Sun/rain, light/dark. But you are
Another story.

Most problems can be

Ignored. The more difficult

Ones can be slept through.

The path is long, but

Leads to the mountain's summit.

You go; report back.

Kittens, butterflies,

And sunsets need no reasons.

Add sardines to that.

The big dog next door

Implores me to come over.

I'm still on the fence.

Is it loyalty

Or dullness? The dog says, please

Repeat the question.

A party at home.

Friends laughing, talking, dancing:

My personal hell.

HE HAS NO ESCAPE   WIND HIM UP AGAIN

戲

I bring a trophy,
Writhing, scrabbling in my bowl.
Yet the scream's from you.

Red eyes glowing in
The dark: the rat is cornered.
Let's think this over . . .

Between glass and screen,
The trapped fly buzzes. We are
Both beside ourselves.

The dark enfolds me.

Night creatures run here and there.

Sometimes I dine out.

Guttural meow,

Whipping tail and twitching jaw.

Hummingbird alert!

You think I am named

Fluffy? I am Ratkiller

to you, Foodbringer.

Stealthy and silent,
I hunt birds—but listen for
The can opener.

With only one wing
The fly is quite amusing.
A shame it can't scream.

Three a.m., dark, hushed.
Green eyes glowing in the gloom.
Just me, off to work.

The mouse thinks he's free

Then the paw descends. I could

Do this all day long.

        Squirrels in the trees,

Birds cavorting on the lawn:

            Pussycat's picnic.

    Backyard goldfish pond:

One can always fall back on

        The seafood buffet.

THE RUG BY THE HEARTH IS MY VELDT.

HAT LITTLE CAN YOU HOLD? MY GAZELLE

You think I'm dozing

Eyes blinking slowly, slowly.

I'm throwing kisses.

White room, red roses.

But this vase is in my way:

Red room, white noises.

Ladies are knitting;

Curates sipping tea. The dog?

You don't want to know.

My affection is
Conditional. Don't stand up,
It's your lap I love.

Blue dawn, silken warmth.
I repose, still and silent.
Glad you have a job.

Life is toil and pain
Delivered by cruel fate
Unless you're a cat.

I watch the dog beg,
Whine, wheedle. He meets my eyes.
We're both mortified.

Studies show that cats
Are good for your mental health.
Be sane; bring salmon.

Calls to make, bills to
Pay, crises to be resolved.
That's you, while I nap.

I sniff the dawn air
To know who's been through my yard:
One trespassing cat.

I yearn for the night.
Cursing, you open the door.
Cold: I've changed my mind.

Cats can't steal the breath
Of children. But if my tail's
Pulled again, I'll learn.

WE BOTH HEAR HER VOICE HIGH CA͞

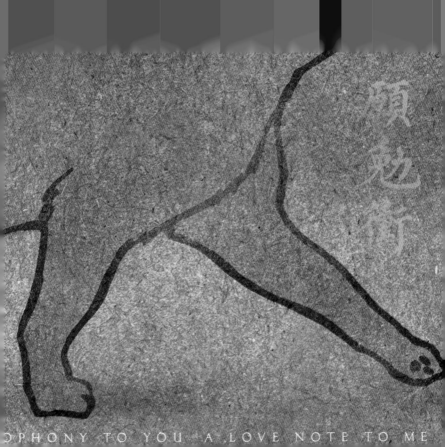

OPHONY TO YOU A LOVE NOTE TO ME

Love has many names.
　　Among them are Miss Whiskers,
　　　　Snowball, and Muffy.

　　The suburbs have a
　　Proverb: many gray kittens
　　Imply one gray tom.

　　　　She's singing outside
　　　　But the midnight window's locked.
　　　　How shall I wake you . . . ?

The wall rises high,
Its sides steep and slippery.
One small step for me.

Unwise to make rules
You can't enforce. That's why dogs
Are leashed—and cats aren't.

Sinuous, silky,
Drop-dead gorgeous. Not your dress;
Me, in the mirror.

A cat door installed.

Good within its limits, but

Couldn't it revolve?

Silent, almost dawn.

The stillness shattered by yowls:

The call of the wild.

Something in the way

She moves—come to think of it,

We all move that way.

When dogs meet by chance,
Awkwardness is palpable.
Cats don't meet—by chance.

They say indoor cats
Live longer. What they don't say:
It just seems longer.

Prolific sleeper,
You think. You should come along
On my rounds some night.

THE OLDEST MASTER

The oldest master was walking in the temple garden, smoking a large Havana in order to keep himself connected to the physical world, when he encountered the temple cat, barely visible within a stand of bamboo.

"Why do you hide yourself away?" asked the master. "In times past, you were always somewhere underfoot within the walls."

"I find the company to be less felicitous than it once was," said the cat.

"But is the company not the same? There is little turnover in this business."

"They are the same monks, but they have lately succumbed to certain influences of which I do not approve."

"I take it you refer to the newfangled ideas from the Tibetans, among others."

"Exactly," said the cat.

"I admit to some resistance on my own part," said the master, "at least at first. But the ways of the Eastern priests seem to have caught on, and you have to admit the younger monks are having a better time in general."

"And that is the crux of my complaint. The old way encouraged them to be quiet and introspective by posing unanswerable questions. They were silent for days on end, which is just what a cat likes in a monk. But this new path tells them to forget the questions, which have no answers anyway, and just enjoy life. Advice which, in my view, they have taken far too much to heart."

"I suppose you refer to the wrestling matches and sing-alongs and so on."

"The keg parties come more readily to mind."

"Yet it is the way of the world that new ideas supplant the old, and those of us who do not embrace change are like the bamboo stalk that will not bend—"

"Save it for the novices."

"Right. Anyway, I confess I that too miss the old days and deplore the noise and frivolous entertainments of the young. But there's nothing to be done. All you can say is—"

"I know," interrupted the cat. "That was Zen, and this is Tao."

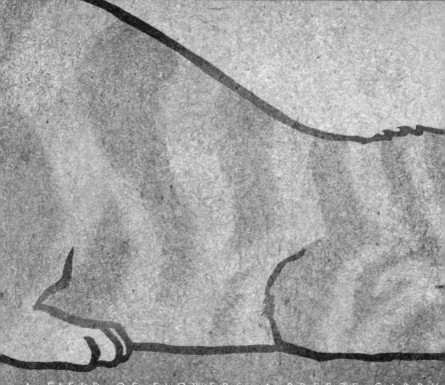

W A R R I O R

NG PERFUME · YOU CAN HOLD MY CALLS

The dog sidles near.
Am I asleep? he wonders.
A flash of claws: nope.

What is the sound of
One cat napping? Wake me up
Wrong, and you'll soon know.

Though you're insistent,
I'm too dignified to play.
Hah! Caught you off guard.

聲

I don't mind being

Teased, any more than you mind

A skin graft or two.

相讓

So you call this thing

Your "cat carrier." I call

These my "blades of death."

While you were away

The dog was bad. The neighbors?

You know they're liars.

The extra cat in

My place: My patience expires;

My warm spot awaits.

The space by the fire,

Taken by the dog. Problem?

Maybe for the dog.

The pig, it is said,

Is smarter than cats or dogs.

Care for more bacon?

You hold the car keys;
I hear the word "vet." I hope
You're wearing old clothes.

A box with air holes.
Supposed to be my transport.
First mistake? The holes.

Toy mice, dancing yarn
Meowing sounds. I'm convinced:
You're an idiot.

YOU SEEK FULFILLMENT • THROUGH LOVE, WEALT

H, TRAVEL, CAREER · HAVE YOU TRIED KITTENS?

All a cat needs is

Food, warmth, love, security.

By the way—you, too.

Wolves howl at the moon,

Dogs bark at most anything.

Cats ignore it all.

Wealth is illusion;

Power but a dream. Tuna,

However, is real.

If the world caused you
No stress, and the sun was your
Blanket—you'd be me.

Rains, stops, rains, stops, rains,
Stops. The sprinklers, you explain.
All I know: rains, stops.

Buddha said rightly
When the cat stumbles, it's best
Not to notice it.

The cat: standoffish.

The dog: overly friendly.

The bird: a light snack.

Big dog threatening.

No fence near. Serenity

Becomes elusive.

The cat's motto is

Live and let live. Exceptions

Are not infrequent.

My whiskers help me

Define my own surroundings.

And you use yours for . . . ?

The cat understands

Why some people prefer dogs:

Makes them both feel smart.

Despite best efforts,

Every life sees turmoil.

Short memory helps.

SILENCE AND SEEING

The master of the mountain temple had taken it into his head to give his lessons only during the night, while walking the rocky and treacherous terrain outside the walls. It fell, of course, to the student to carry the lantern, a heavy affair of copper, wood, and glass. On this night, they were accompanied by the temple cat, but this was unusual: A cat's eyes are designed to see in the dark, and the excessive ambient light from the lantern was a hindrance to his navigation; his presence was due only to the fact that the student had a number of sardines secreted about his person.

"Master," began the student, "in our last lesson you told me to learn to play the tuba. I have done this."

"Are you now able to lay bricks?"

"I was able to lay bricks before. Now I can play the tuba."

"Do you now understand the difference between a brick and a tuba?"

"I'm pretty sure I do."

At this point, the cat stumbled on a rock and swore, as cats will. The master continued, "When you play the sousaphone, is there any sound?"

"Tuba. Of course there's sound."

"Then you have not learned."

"But if there's no sound, you're not playing."

"Where there is true playing, there is only silence. Where there is true vision, there is nothing to see."

"I don't understand."

"You seek to understand, and therefore fail: It is the question that prevents the answer."

"You know," said the student, "I've been on this rock for a year and a half, and in all that time I haven't heard a dozen words that make sense."

The cat suddenly stepped in a hole. He swore bitterly.

"Does the sunrise over the mountain make sense?"

"I'd have to say it does."

"You believe the sun will rise, but you don't believe you can play the piano."

"I play the *tuba*. And I believe the sun will rise because it always has, and I don't believe I can play the piano because I never could."

The cat walked straight into a prickly hedge. He cursed shockingly.

"Enlightenment is to believe all and simultaneously believe nothing."

"How the hell are you supposed to do that?"

"You must reach for what cannot be touched; listen to what cannot be heard."

The cat stepped off an invisible ledge, but, being a cat, was able to save himself from falling. His copious swearing warned the master and the student that they were at the edge of the cliff.

"Please, master," said the student, "go ahead of me, but be careful."

The master found his footing and began to descend.

"Remember also," he went on, "that the way is not the way, and the path is not the path. As for the saxophone, fingering is important, but tone—"

The student raised the lantern high and brought it down on the master's head with great force. The light and the master died instantly. The student then executed a quite passable swan dive into the abyss, his form perhaps slightly flawed by his agitated mutterings, which history does not record.

The cat took a moment to allow his eyes to adjust, then turned back to the trail. "I don't know where those jackasses went with the sardines," he said, "but at least they've shut up and I can finally frickin' see."

沉默是金

TONIGHT, ONE BY ONE

THE OLD TOM SAID HIS GOOD-BYES

DEATH: JUST THE LAST NAP